PIANO ACCOMPANIMENT

More Folk Strings

Piano Accompaniment
Arranged and Edited by Joanne Martin

CONTENTS

Shoo Fly	2
Tancuj, Tancuj	5
Linstead Market	8
Un canadien errant	10
Bella Bimba	12
The Leaving of Liverpool	13
I've Been Working on the Railroad	16
Auprès de ma blonde	18
Good Evening	20
Sakura	22

Cover Design: Candy Woolley
Illustrations: Rama Hughes

© 2003 Summy-Birchard Music
division of Summy-Birchard Inc.
All Rights Reserved   Printed in U.S.A.

ISBN 1-58951-172-7

Summy-Birchard Inc.
exclusively distributed by
Warner Bros. Publications
15800 NW 48th Avenue
Miami, Florida 33014

Any duplication, adaptation or arrangement of the compositions contained in this collection requires the written consent of the Publisher.
No part of this book may be photocopied or reproduced in any way without permission. Unauthorized uses are an infringement of the U.S. Copyright Act and are punishable by law.

SHOO FLY

United States
Arranged by JOANNE MARTIN

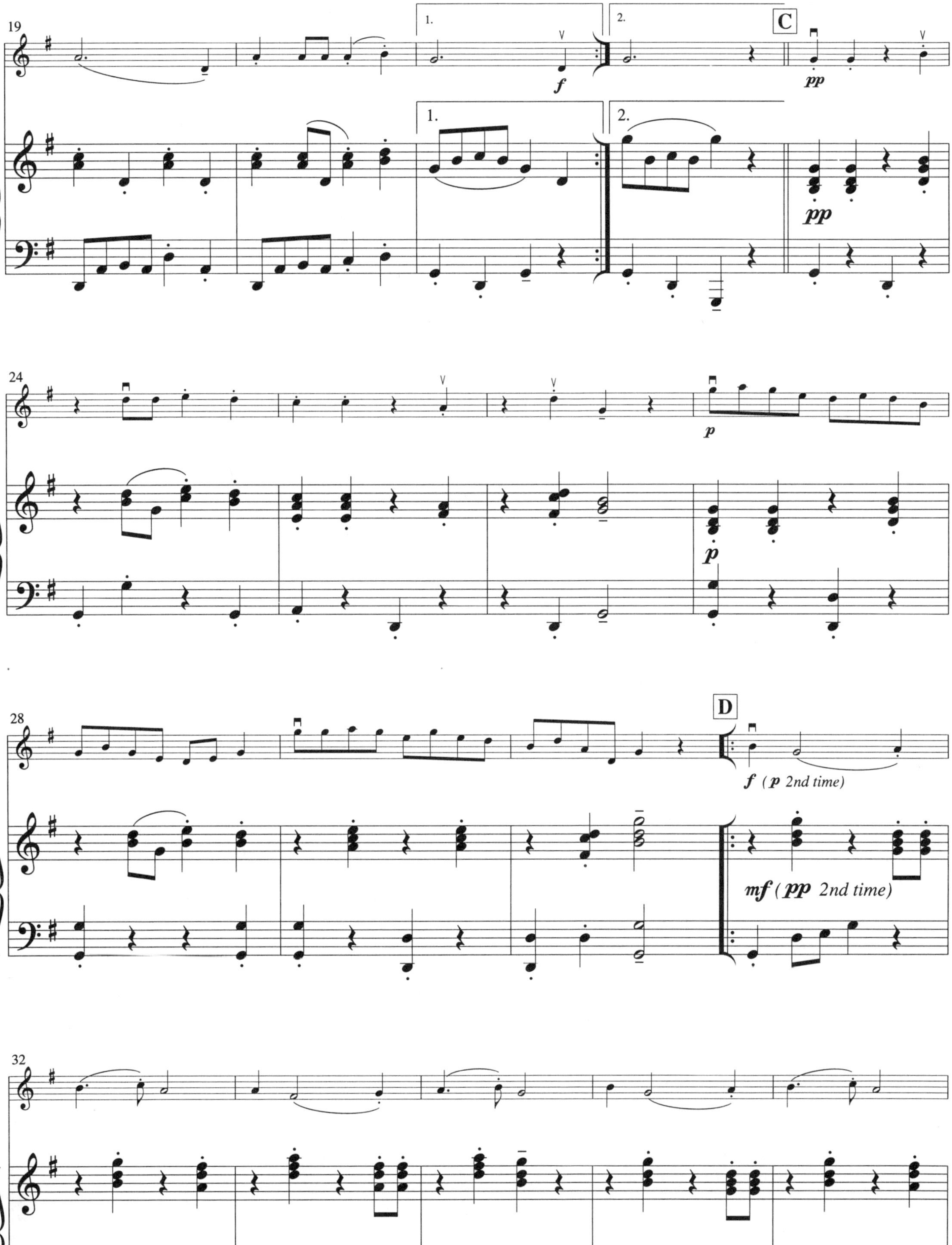
19
1.
2.
C
f
pp
24
p
28
D
f (p 2nd time)
mf (pp 2nd time)
32

37
1.
2.
E
f
(ff 2nd time)
8va 2nd time
mf (f 2nd time)
41
(8va)
45
ff
F
pp
50
cresc.
f
8va

TANCUJ, TANCUJ

Slovakia
Arranged by JOANNE MARTIN

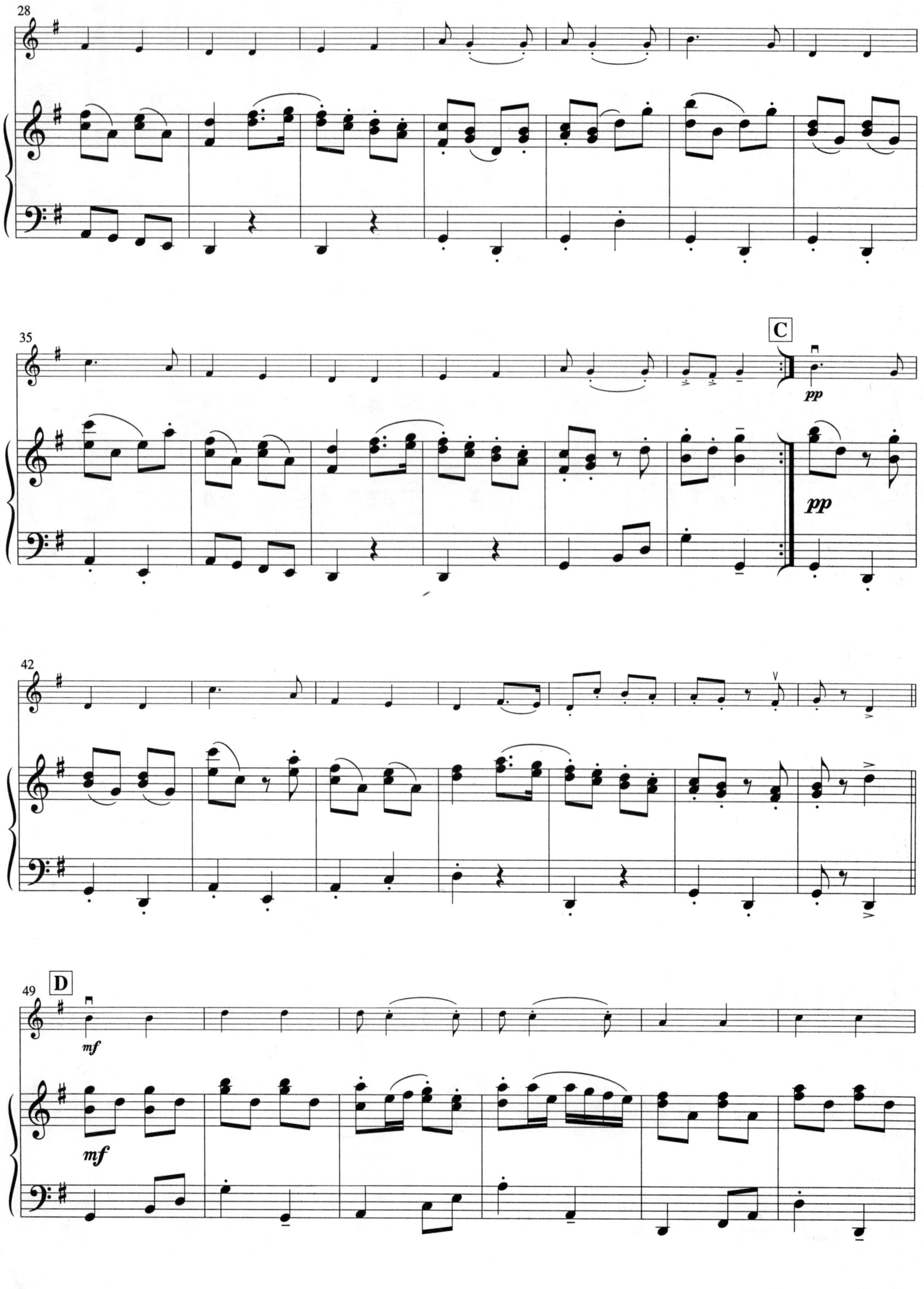
28
35
C
pp
pp
42
49
D
mf
mf

Tancuj, tancuj - 3

LINSTEAD MARKET

Jamaica
Arranged by JOANNE MARTIN

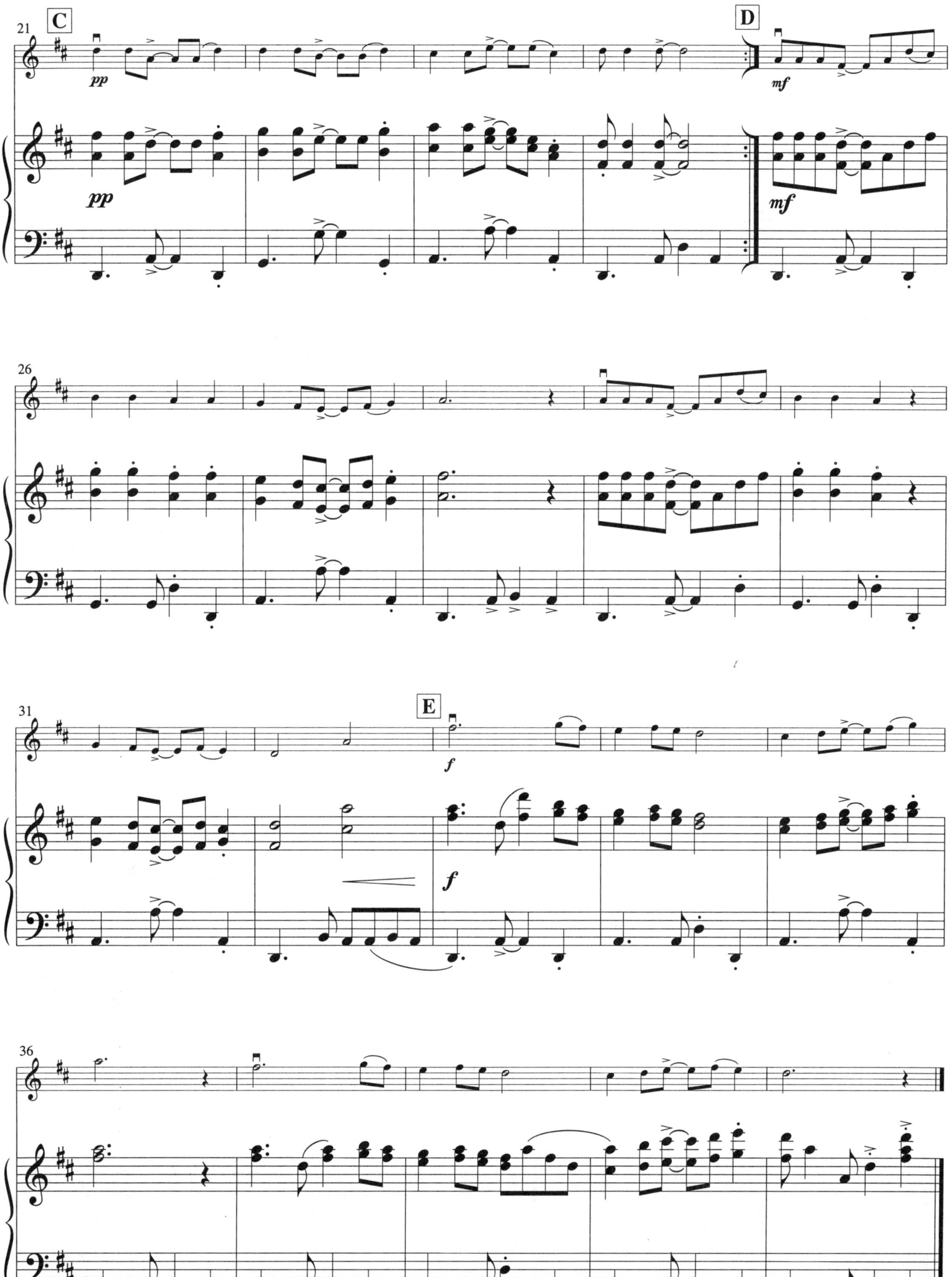
21
C
pp
D
mf
26
31
E
f
36

UN CANADIEN ERRANT

Canada
Arranged by JOANNE MARTIN

40
D
mp
p
pp
50
E
mp
p
60
F
f
mf
mp
p
70
dim. poco a poco
pp
dim. poco a poco
pp

BELLA BIMBA

Italy
Arranged by JOANNE MARTIN

THE LEAVING OF LIVERPOOL

England
Arranged by JOANNE MARTIN

10
B
f
mf
14
mf
mp
18
C
poco rit.
pp
a tempo
poco rit.
pp
a tempo
23
D
mp
p

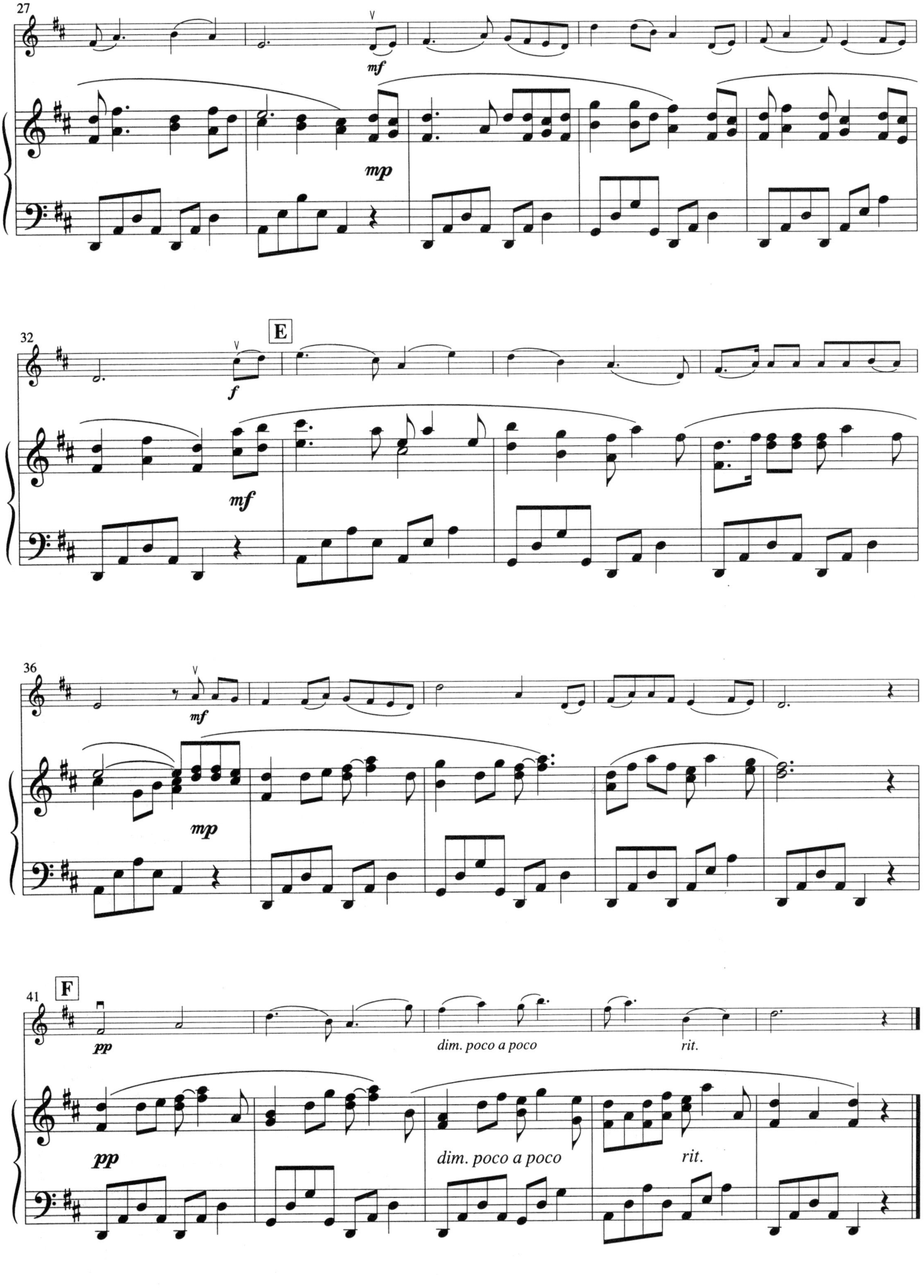
27
mf
mp
32
E
f
mf
36
mf
mp
41
F
pp
dim. poco a poco
rit.

I'VE BEEN WORKING ON THE RAILROAD

United States
Arranged by JOANNE MARTIN

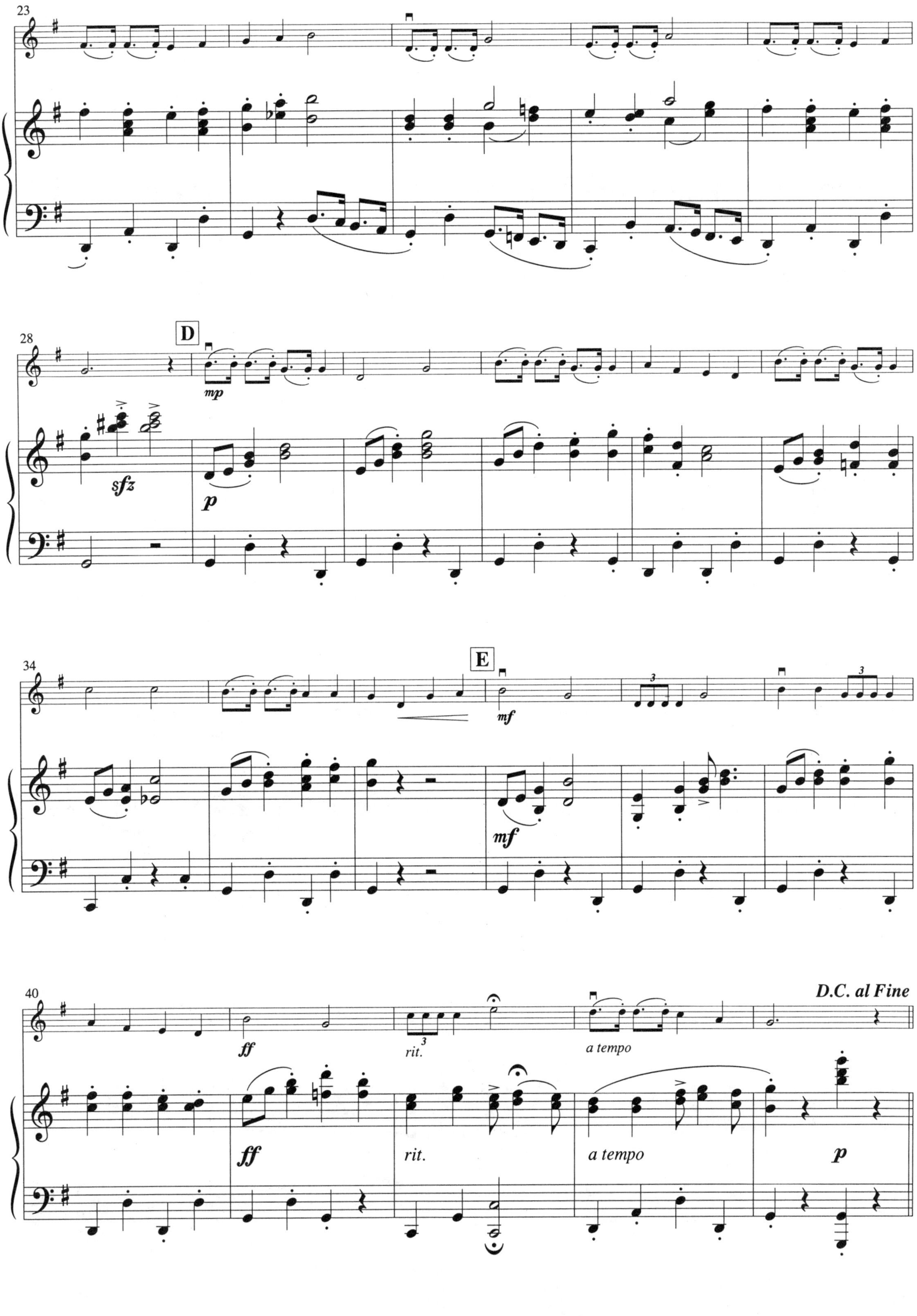
23
28
D
mp
sfz
p
34
E
mf
40
D.C. al Fine
ff
rit.
a tempo

AUPRÈS DE MA BLONDE

Canada
Arranged by JOANNE MARTIN

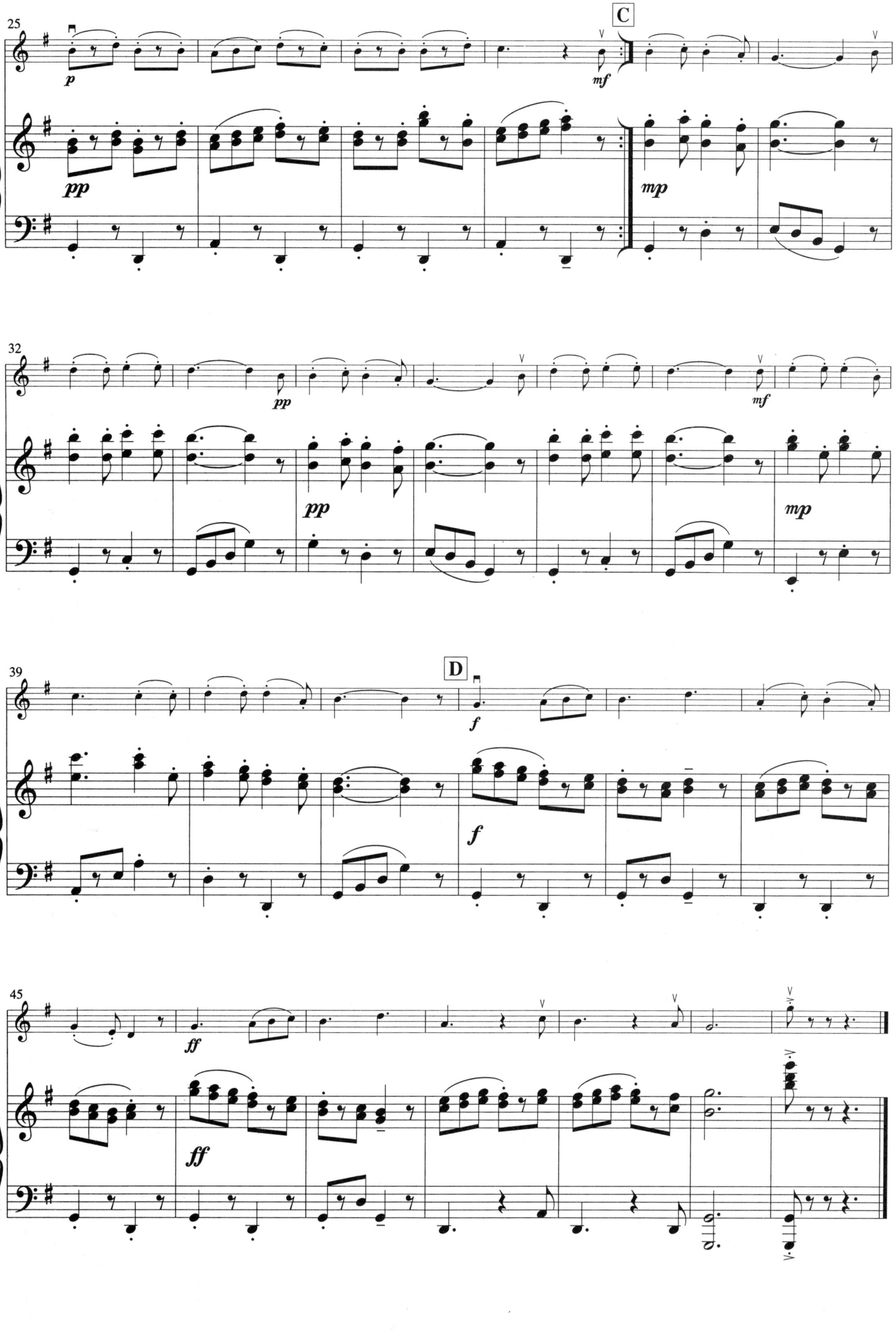
25
p
pp
C
mf
mp
32
pp
pp
mf
mp
39
D
f
f
45
ff
ff

GOOD EVENING

Denmark
Arranged by JOANNE MARTIN

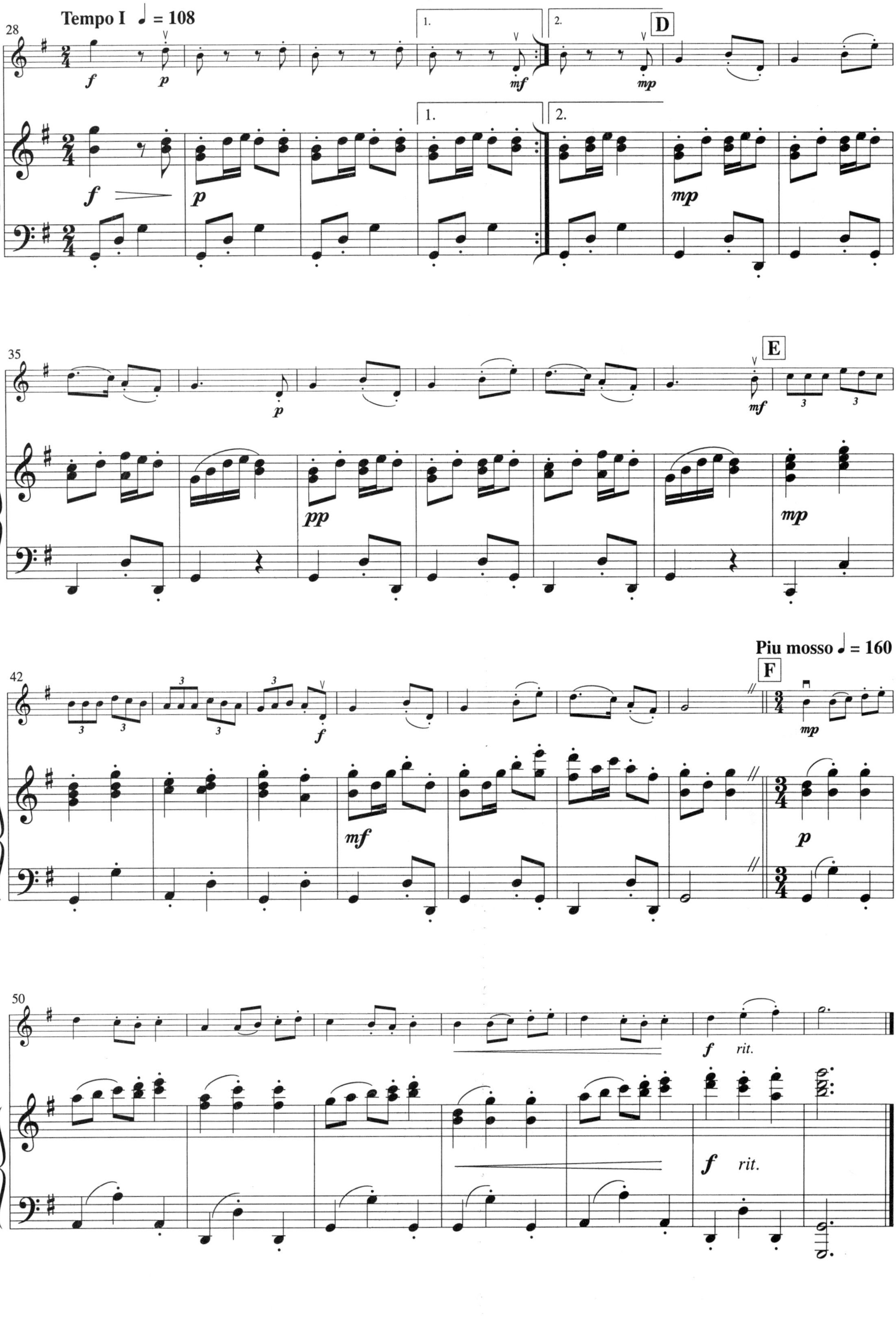
28
Tempo I ♩ = 108
1.
2.
D
35
E
42
Piu mosso ♩ = 160
F
50
rit.
rit.

SAKURA

Japan
Arranged by JOANNE MARTIN

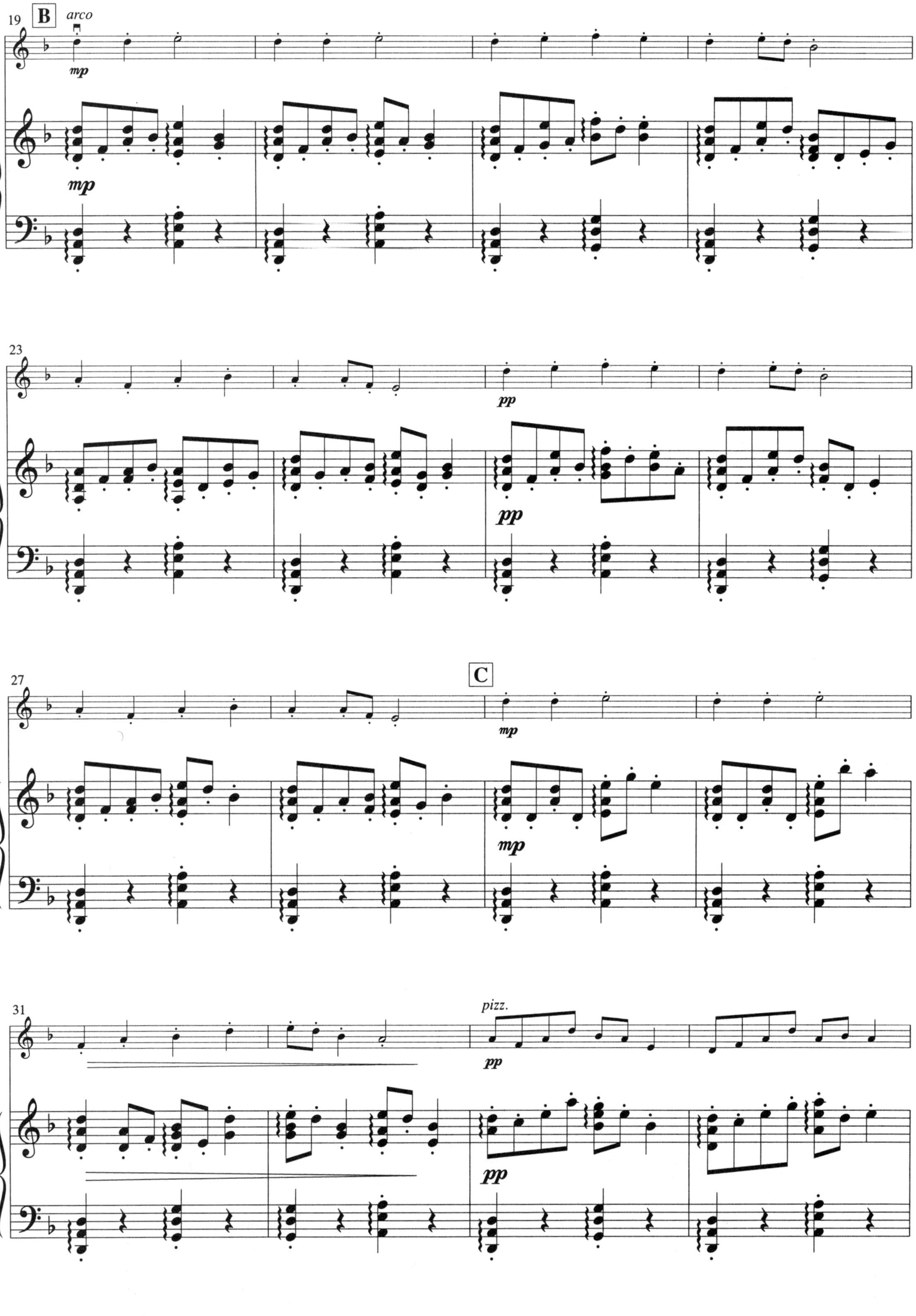
19
B
arco
mp
mp
23
pp
pp
27
C
mp
mp
31
pizz.
pp
pp

24 Sakura - 3